Luna Moth

and other poems

STEVE LUXTON

Luna Moth
and other poems

LIVRES
DC
BOOKS

Cover illustration by Geneviève Côté.
Book designed and typeset in Adobe Garamond Pro
and Myriad MM by Primeau & Barey, Montreal.

Printed and bound in Canada by AGMV Marquis.
Distributed by Lit DistCo.

Legal Deposit, Bibliothèque nationale du Québec
and the National Library of Canada, 4th trimester, 2004.

Library and Archives Canada Cataloguing in Publication
Luxton, Steve, 1946–
Luna moth and other poems / Steve Luxton.

ISBN 0-919688-92-6 (bound).–ISBN 0-919688-91-8 (pbk.)
I. Title.
PS8573.U98L84 2004 C811'.54 C2004-905938-6

DC Books gratefully acknowledges the support
of The Canada Council for the Arts, The Book
Publishing Industry Development Program
of the Department of Canadian Heritage, and
of SODEC for our publishing program.

Canada Council for the Arts
Conseil des Arts du Canada

Société de développement des entreprises culturelles
Québec

DC Books
950 Decarie, Box 662
Montreal, Quebec, H4L 4V9
www.dcbooks.ca

In memory of my
father Colin Luxton and
of Louis Dudek

Thanks also for help and advice
and inspiration to Robert Allen,
Keith Henderson, Ber Lazarus,
Susan Palmer, Todd Swift and
many others.

Contents

1 To My Dying Father
2 At the Dawn Window, a Luna Moth
3 Silver Whiskers
5 The Remedy of Art
7 Untitled
8 Infant Visits the Neurological Ward
9 Rogue Affinities
11 Fay
13 Departure
14 Post-operative Ode
15 Guided Tour of the JFK Presidential Assassination Theme Park
20 New England Playbill
21 Sleeping in the Country House Parlor
22 The Angler Re-connects
24 Last Good Talk
26 To See a Bull Moose
28 Boreal Phantasmagoria
30 A Dream: the Prince and the Pauper
31 Millennial Suspense, February 1999
32 At the Office
33 Voyage to the Heian
35 Burger Joint Sex Fantasy
36 Post Epic
37 Letter of Support to a Beleaguered American President

39 What the U.S. Action Hero Needs
41 While Doing My Exercises
42 Blues Funk
44 Redneck Genesis
45 The End of Our World
46 Jack Sprat and His Wife
47 The Helots
48 Chicago Harp Blues
50 Spider Bend
51 Nihil Admirari
52 September Campfire on the Gouin Reservoir
53 This Life
55 On the Subject of the Non-existence of Matter
56 Ornithological Mystery
57 Dark Asteroid
58 Big Nose Kate, Lover of Doc Holliday, Reminisces
61 Battle Site, Minnesota
65 Ur Cur
66 The Ballad of Doc Holliday
68 Dad
70 Tantrums
72 The Night before D-Day
73 To Hazel Walker
75 The Indescribability of Fear
76 After the Operation: First Visitor
78 Last Commando on His Deathbed

To My Dying Father

You might have picked me up more.
I hardly recall your touch,
though one Sunday, when I was four,
in our small back garden, under brief British sun,
you clipped a flat top on the seven-foot hedge,
and suddenly hoisted me to the very top,
up close to the mottled, uncertain sky,
left me there, out from under your feet
while you attended to other tasks.
I must have cried in fear, though I'm not sure,
rather I remember the great animate shuddering
  of the privet
like a vast stiff brush beneath, a rolling wave,
myriad rough palms and elbows
that could not quite agree to hold me
or shrug me helpless off.
I felt such abandonment to terror and delight
and for the first time glimpsed at that huge height
the entire world.

At the Dawn Window, a Luna Moth

Ravishing ephemera,
oblivion's Winged Victory,
between this pane and the red sun
you tilt enchanting pinions,
Great Awk-ward.

We are (I am)
though barely yet awake,
rapt at each other,
limbs circumfluent,
optic stalks in a pother,
two blended powders
of the first blue air.

Greetings fabulous aeronaut!
Sister, brother: none other,
your whorls are the very
white works of our
scattering galaxy.

In your eyes I see,
and in your pinched
bog-man's face,
life's matchless,
brief rich penury.

Silver Whiskers

"The purpose of animal whiskers
    is to gauge crawl-space widths."

Sepulchered a year
in a cedar bough hole,
this mink
waxes pharaonic.

Gone the feline sinews,
the lithe flesh,
fattened on mice and trout,
then spring-water slaked,
molted the furrier's plume,
once svelte ermine.

Rigid on my palm,
mighty Cheops in miniature,
grave-robbed,
time-stiffened,
plundered,
except for marvelous,
intact, silver whiskers.

Re-interring you in your niche,

late-potentate,
I get the message
of your immortal crypt:
strait is the gate.

You were despot of this swamp,
yet life was still
wriggle and squeeze
through low portals
and long tunnels with small width.

The Remedy of Art

After the shot, I morph myself into a creature
armed to the gills against residual agony.
This night, I elect to be a crab.
Step-by-step, I imagine my inflamed pulp-and-jelly
molded over by formidable armoured sections:
breast-plate, pauldrons. I suspect
around me, despite the painkillers
broadcast freely throughout the ward,
not all my fellow patients are so adaptive.

The night quickly becomes disturbed,
disturbing: naked howling erupts,
moaning, screaming. Tightly, I curl in bed,
swivel my buttocks, turn my back
towards the worst of the racket.
Minutes later, the nurse drops by,
carrying what I requested: a radio.

Slow or quick jazz now swells,
Bechet, Beiderbecke, Holliday.
Squeezing my eyes shut, I'm now Crab:
scrambling after gusts,
whiffs of cool and lovely sound,

a beach away from agony's raw sea,
up across sun-tortured dunes till, finally,
past the steep seawall, under a boardwalk,
in a niche beneath a dodgy roof of tumbled
blocks and winding, knotted reinforcing rods,
I hunch, twitch, concentrate on sublime notes.

My eyes, though firmly sealed,
flood with the difference between shade
and brightness, the mottled ghosts of a corroded,
massive, sunlit, underside of chaos,
blinding chrome points splintering off
a giant distant parking lot of highly polished,
unrecognizably fantastic,
red and gold upholstered convertibles.

Untitled

Falling straight down, rain
makes tight rings in the river pool,
framed by wider, eddying spheres
where shore willows release vast drops....

May my poems be like these:
loaded by clouds into wild tops,
gathered and converged by countless
  twigs and leaves,
then released, full of the sky's
  grey-gold palette,
the taste off ancient trees.

Infant Visits the Neurological Ward

Smooth skulled as
nearly all the rest of us,
pink-faced and as given
to sudden weeping,
but with life ahead
long as your father's scalp scar
or pretty mother's look,
small treasure to so many
sad watching eyes.

Rogue Affinities

Unmindful of the reich-lord's
record of immitigable murder,
oblivious to the Victor's apportioning
the bluff fellow his due for the twentieth
century's most sanguinary butchery,
the American guard at Spandau,
delighted to discover a fellow *bon vivant,*
profound lover of fine food, liquors,
silver chased sporting weapons,
slipped a poison capsule to Herr
Hermann Goering,
thus permitting an unpityingly genial
war criminal to escape The Rope.

Far past midnight in Spandau gaol
waltzed conversations between
the Lederhosen
and the outdoorsy Ohio Buckeye,

palates and bellies love-lacing the bars
just before he palmed the pill:
an almond flavoured aperitif.

Great fools men can sometimes be,
so wrongheaded and susceptible
to misguided sympathies and blundering
compassion.
What can be done in the face of such
incorrigible empathy?

Fay

Things one loves most
rarely have the time for each other:
have you noticed?

Usher her,
the lovely Dolores of your wildest dreams,
to your secret, red-watered, salmonid pool,

note unhappily how as you hymn the riffle,
her matchless eyes
perceptibly drift sideways,

then away,
(unless you proffer a gracious comparison)
though later when your *Grande Affaire*'s passé

she'll remind you
(in the spirit of friendly solidarity)
about that wonderful, unforgettable

hiking and fishing trip.
She'll be unable to recall exactly
where the sublime brook rushed

nor has a moment right now
for you to refresh her recall,
though every time you still wander there,

her lovely absence haunts the spot
like a svelte wild trout,
twirling and glittering,

uncatchable,
in exile from her own memory,
still deep in yours,

witch of a lonesome watery-glade,
fey, rising to the soaked
long-tailed fly of your sadness.

Departure

Kissing the headrest of my dead father's chair,
embracing at the door, then waving slow goodbye
to my barely ambulatory mum,
I step out on the lurid, watery street to find
my car poked way out onto the road's crown.

How could I have parked so badly?
Then I remember. Somewhat akimbo,
at each end of the sole available spot,
far off the curb, two vehicles already stood,
each leaving me only peculiar, oblique room.

One's driven off now; the other's just going.
Thus my crazy jut: rear-end up on the sidewalk
before my parent's condo, front protruding,
wheels wrenched back like a kid's stroller,
axles seized, forever abandoned.

Post-operative Ode

The smiling, big-domed neurosurgeon
at my bedside said he'd popped
the tumor off my brain
like a cherry off a sundae.

Spiked with plenty of codeine,
prostrate under oxygen mask and drip-gear,
I envisioned an ungainly black,
rune-inscribed bead wedged,
pinched down my nostril
by glittering long-shanked tweezers,

maybe a green, brightly glowing
alien implant extracted
with a bedstead cracking spasm and yell,
something more dramatic than
a date at the Dairy Queen!

"Do you need a nurse?" the Doctor blandly adds.
When I nod rhythmically,
he beckons to a white clad waitress,
turns away, but pledges to return quite soon,
in a voice mellifluous and smooth
as coned ice cream that this time at least,
did not topple off onto the sidewalk.

Guided Tour of the JFK Presidential Assassination Theme Park

For Rob Allen

Outside gleaming, Detroit-limo black, plastic walls,
In Megalopolitan Dallas,
On an ebony ramp to the towering portal,
Hucksters of all kinds snatch at your sleeves.
(We tolerate touts and beggars.)
They cajole, harangue you from their booths,
Pitching 3-D portraits digitally daubed
On velvet, Kennedy masks, antique secret service
Saigon shades, Oswald's newly discovered,
(Possibly genuine) secret journal,
Purported fragments of the true projectile,
Of Massachusetts Adonis' tonsure,
Blurry snaps of FBI Hoover in a tutu,
Slipping a Manlicher-Carcano to a Havana Mafioso.

Inside the inner wall,
(Look! Cinderblocks from Berlin!)
The thousand acre compound,
Greater than the old World Trade Center,
Contains an entire assassination "location,"
A mile of four-lane, some industrial real-estate,
A score of intersections, swooping ramps,

Deck-topped office buildings, all installed
With accessorized bays at every sniper position–

Fantasy assassin, wait your turn!

There, at the park's huge center
Looms the great museum proper,
Layered wedding cake design
To recall the old White House,
(Micro-nuked decades back
By Finnish-American Odinists),
Now morphed into Tintagel Castle,
Camelot's suspected site,
With text-based resources and piles
Of glossy pictures, you might say
Le Louvre of Kennedy necrophilia.
Had she been cryogenically sustained,
Jackie would have liked it a whole lot!

Equal-handedly, it presents the case,
Accompanied by full, hyper-realistic,
Three dimensional simulation,
For every known conspiracy theory
The hue and cry industry has unearthed.
This encyclopedic labyrinth fills a Pentagon,

Climaxed in hushed far-reaches, at the very heart,
By round-the-block line-ups,
With a virtual booth (holographic) permitting you,
Mr. & Mrs. America, to re-enact the personal,
Hands-on homicide of the Chief Executive.

If you choose, you may relive
The attempted Oswald escape
Through the brilliant, cooling Sixties
Suburbs of Dallas, blasting *en passant* a clueless cop
Before ducking into movie house darkness,
Getting trapped: at the Texas police station,
Whoremaster Ruby's outstretched payback pistol....

An opportunity for vicarious victimology!

Later, outside the exit, you may visit
An officially unsanctioned private booth
Where (for a modest fee) you can be patched
Into the news photo of Oswald crumpling,
Or Ruby, or into the shocked crowd
In the Abraham Zapruder film; again
(For a few extra dollars) grimace,
Jerk sideways in front of the doomed president,

Playing Governor Connolly!
Or on Air Force One, smiling in shy complicity,
Giving your boy, Lyndon, the oath!

Just beyond the official exhibition center,
Maybe a hundred yards or so,
The actual kill-site awaits,
Terraplaned amphitheatrical for improved
Photography, (notice the winking bed
Of dummy rifle-impact lights),
The precise historic spot where
John-of-Camelot was gloriously raised up,
Source of so much inspiration.
Despite all, it remains almost exactly as it was,
As does, thirty yards on, the notorious
Grassy knoll and overpass!
Yes, the berm's abandoned, neglected
Condition may surprise you,
However the spot's spontaneously grown
Into an American Hyde Park Corner,
Featuring round the clock democratic debate,
Complete (for safety's sake)
With concealed weapons detectors and razor-wire fence.

Tour's up: there's the exit!

Just time to post your thoughts
To our theory chat-room.
A representative sample follows.

You too can be next!

Folks, this is actually the century's second
Great *tremendo mistero.* The first:
D'you know much about old Russia –
The Tsar and his family's murder?
And of mad Rasputin, their advisor?
They've finally found the family bones,
Including Anastasia's....
Odd though, the heir Alexander's weren't there.
He was the one survived,
Hemophiliac, spoke good English, about the same age
As the purportedly Addisonian Jack Kennedy,
Who lied about both his ailment and his age....
A no-brainer, huh? So the Commies
And our Big Boys took the young pres out,
independently.
Two huge squads of pro shooters
(Ignorant of each other), simultaneously.
Pop-pop! Pop-pop-pop-pop-

From every conceivable building and direction!

New England Playbill

I'm driving alone far too late
through northern Vermont wilds.
Wet upland snow turns the highway
into botched sheet-music,
mostly blank pages,
few visible staves or clefs.

Eyes strain, hands throb,
as buried ridges rear everywhere,
my only company the dashboard radio.
I've long given up trying to listen to one station,
relinquishing selection and reception
to successive glimpsed mountains.

That clear-cut hump picks "Golden Oldies,"
a slimmer peak, a trembling nocturne.
Trailing her white ballroom scarf,
that farther ample Dame chooses
Les Brown's Band of Renown
featuring a young and winsome Doris Day.

The blizzard goes pink then blue.
Till dawn the lonesome mountains play me
their sentimental favourites, then let me through.

Sleeping in the Country House Parlor

My woman's gone: so forget
sleeping lonely in the upstairs double!
I'll make my camp before the stove.
What a strange, shadowy, off-trail formation,
weird brush, stark garage-sale furnishings,
angular bric-a-brac lamp....
And now the lights off, me rolled in my bag,
what odd sounds from critters!
Howls from half-wolves next door,
crawl-space coon squeaks,
a porcupine gnawing at plywood glue,
like a slow buzz saw,
closer yet, on the turntable,
the needle at the end of an old LP,
pounding, pounding
like a mad trapper at my cabin door.

The Angler Re-connects

Blinded again by water-beauty,
I seem to forget, like love,
trout fishing demands
deft approach and presentation.

Semi-tufted nub, my head's silhouette,
broaches the pool.
My rod's whip follows, slicing
across the stream's swift lights.

Still stalking,
eyes out for slick stones,
feet hopping mauve-brown holes,
I spot the flitting of a tell-tale shadow!

Trout darting below,
bird crossing above?
Eyes heavenwards, I go down full length,
just in time grab my fly-away glasses.

Now the trout are out of their holes!
Hauling myself out, dripping,
confirmed klutz and still growing,
I crouch on a big birdlimed boulder,

thinking maybe this is no longer
a profitable expenditure of my time,
when suddenly I miss my wallet.
No, it's here still, dry but empty.

Then I spot my money, my identity card,
plus all its lurid plastic kin, flocking
to that wonderful multi-coloured shindig
in the sunlit whirlpool downstream.

Last Good Talk

Before I fly back East,
my father and I unexpectedly stay up.
Fate, at long last, has
arranged a personal interview.

We converse, later chat finally
about life's extremities:
him sixty years ago in a rubber dinghy
stalking an enemy shore.
I describe in detail how,
canoe-tripping, I failed to save
a drug-crazed Tacoma guy
who flipped out of his powerful
inboard, likely trying to ram me.

And about how, not too long ago,
in the brain-tumor ward,
the fellow in the next bed lunged,

shrieking "Who the fuck am I?"
Pulled me out of bed
and with our tubes almost throttled me.
(Fending him off, I could hardly remember who *I* was.)

Emptying his beer with a sigh,
dad hauls limping out to the kitchen,
comes back with more.
The night's session goes on and on,
between us, no struggle any more!
He faces Death again, for good,
knows I've almost been there:
my fate's sealed too.
Outdone both, our last laugh is shared.

To See a Bull Moose

Forget it!
Then walk low, wet country,
distracted from the usual civilized distractions
by, say, the disembodied wig of foam twirling on a riffle,
rough swathe in the grass left
by a slouching snapping turtle.

Come to the farthest
reach of your planned walk
then fretfully turn, in your head too,
facing again the usual concerns:
unanswered e-mails,
fatty diet, taxes, death.

Soon, it is like someone upstream
blew the big old beaver dam,
floating the sky-high pile in the barn
through the kitchen into the bedroom!
Worry some more, stop noticing anything,
talk to yourself out loud, at odds,
certainly not watching your step,
so that raving away on a ravine slope,

you trip, roll cursing out
onto a long, naked river shoal,
where once, crisp with hope, you trout fished but got bit,
fetch up beside a clay-bank, fever orange jewel-weed,
oddly shaped spikes of driftwood,
a sucker corpse gone putrid.

Suddenly a bull moose, not thirty paces off,
eight feet tall, head burdened by
a redundant craze of antlers, swung your way,
now long-legging it slowly east,
face dolorous, curious, like the slow,
long nosed, kindly deacon who once discovered you,
bright kid with a sure thing future, fallen
spread-eagled at the foot of playground steps,
bloody-kneed, dazed, unsure of where he was.

Boreal Phantasmagoria

On the river trail past dark
a phosphor moon
in fresh snow-piled
deadfalls... runes!

I am deciphering
difficult silver texts
when, brushed with frost,
a fox leaps forth,

folkloric phantom,
snow ploughs down a drift,
looks back once, skidding,
darts upstream on the
first edge of winter ice.

Seized, unable to divine
that jagged red gaze,
I halt on the trail,
when, with a tinkle-crash,
edged like fantastic green-blue glass,

a piece of ice (split off),
comes floating dead-silent by,
fresh Antarctic raft,
the fox ice-borne,
legs splayed,

pointy snout thrust down,
eyes glancing up from under
with another inscrutable intensity,
all the way down
to the next fast bend of the river.

A Dream: the Prince and the Pauper

In my lover's old friend's grand Manhattan place,
daughter of the Queen Mum's late urologist,
who was to boot, one of Britain's
most eminent amateur orientalists,
groggily visiting the immense bathroom before bed,
I sway before a vast mirror trimmed with
diverse glimmering chinoiserie, start shucking
my shirt snake-skin-like over my head.

Blindfolded, I stagger against an unseen niche,
my hands, baffled in their sleeves,
in off-balance terror, clutch, fasten on a pair
of priceless vases, dinosaur-egg heavy, then freeze!
Hooded in hideous darkness, I hunch
smothered by impending disaster,
unforgettable plebian embarrassment,
when in my head a little voice pipes up and tempts:

Go ahead! Drop them! Be Free!
For one moment be *Emperor!*
But it was a dream... and I was me.

Millennial Suspense, February 1999

Walking the Jersey shore off-season at sunset
because my cheap room looks inland,
I return past queues of shuttered coastal motels,
cross a parking lot with one long-shadowed car,
my own, mount the metal stairs and hear
a loud pop–a key support rivet?

Seized in mid-climb, waiting to splatter
onto tomorrow's Front Page,
I slide my eyes upward, and for the first time,
silver finger gouge on a wall of deep blue,
I spot Hale Bop. The stairs bang again!

What a last moment!
His last sight was what he climbed up for:
an explicit Apocalyptic sign, the celebrated comet–
personally tailored End Time!

Then, of course, as usual,
the entirely inscrutable
nothing happened....

At the Office

I camp at my desk, paper-dammed, sighing.
Beyond the ceiling grate, the unseen fan churns
like a river escaping
an impounded, silted watershed.

Here, among leaning book stacks,
an unread two-sheet update
on my forever impending pension,
I do fuck-all,
fritter time away folding
an *origami* canoe light and slim
enough to portage past the vent.

Voyage to the Heian

Yeats, past master, unzip,
bail out of your Byzantine gold foil bird-suit
before it rides your crotch once more.
Aesthete-geek, first laid at twenty-eight,
uncoop from Ecstasy Intellectual's timeless palace:
buy a plane ride, catch a dolphin even
to Cipangu, first millennium Japan.

Yes, get thee to The Heian, celibate Celt!
On the sun-stroked floor of an ancient shinden,
pouts no Dire Dierdre to stew you in your juices,
just a jet-haired damsel to brew you in them
while discretely annotating her "pillow book"
with tanka celebrating your formless utterances.

For in Heian Kyo, love of beauty
and the beauty of love is all.
Man is high-dreaming *and* corporeal.
He quaffs, rhymes (excessively),
string-plucks the white moon,
enters competitive perfume-mixing festivals,
while passionately exchanging intimacies
    of love and state.

A society sentenced to fade away,
laid waste too soon by harsh warrior monks,

still, Billy Y., is intransience all?
Where to tuck one's sacred parts
in such a tightly tailored suit?
What a nest for small birds!

Give me hot saki and hold the sour sponge!

You see, past master, immortality on a twig
has you looking peaked–a morgue's delight.
Accept the invitation from The Shining Prince: Indite!
beside a courtesan muse in a shimmering silk wrap....

'Cause Life is fleeting and immortality's likely crap!

Great tweeter, in Heian Kyo perhaps,
you'll chance, while sucking your quince,
to hear some ancient lyricist,
as he is tippling, moved to cry,
"O, like the waters, all that's beautiful drifts away!"–
expressing your own sense of *Rerum Lacrimae,*
a lovely and bittersweet descant,
decanted (delicately) into the mouth,
till brimming, it soaks the lips and body both.

Burger Joint Sex Fantasy

At fry basket heat
a twin burger plus
two maxi shakes sort of guy
fuses
with his equally obese spouse,

(with a hollow roar)
sucks her up
dreaming fervently of a tastier
straw-slim secretary.

No less short-ordered,
(but savvier about additives)
his wife conjures her own menu substitute,
a patty
of even vaster proportions,

compared to whom,
her distracted mate
is lithe,
buff as an onion ring.

Post Epic

The late Fall wind across my window sill
sounds like Homer's Penelope (or is it The Sirens?)
purring insistently to her Ulysses,
that, after his long sojourn, he perhaps
set forth once more (quickly head out!)
for distant Troy or far-off anywhere,
to that magnificent stack of ruins
(so very often described by him)
where, it is rumoured, despite the storied conflagration,
the great timber horse still rears.
Mane grayed, chiseled thighs withered
by years of rain, sun, long abandonment,
it poses in a wind swirled, ash-edged plaza
while hundreds of ragged fowl
ply its toothless mouth, shunting back and forth
like an old has-been and drunk's
garrulous, ceaselessly carping tongue.

Letter of Support to a Beleaguered American President

You'll never be that hard-bitten shango,
Clint (Eastwood) or another debonair
Harvard hairpiece, boy-God Jack,
That naughty saint. Don't pout:
Life is full of disappointment,
Particularly for the brilliant,
Humble of origin, and pudgy.

You have, as the literary critics say,
Discovered your own unique voice anyway,
Inspired utterance, under that pliant mouth,
Ms. Lewinski's ministrations,
Zoftig intern and bugle-girl, rendering fervent
National service in a White House broom closet.

O you charming rogue you!

With a revived economy and early-dotage yuppies
Secretly reveling in your flaws,
Fat prince of willing trailer park fellatrices,
Cad, dick-head, opportunistic upstart
(Without peer), you grabbed your chance
To baldly go where they would rather:

Wank and wonk, diddle and bonk,
Then outrageously lie, lie, deny, deny!

I did not have sexual relations with that woman!

Anybody who fiddles like you Bill,
Or later, confessing his trespasses,
Sweats with such touching vulnerability
(And contrition), who can give the major
Media networks that sort of a blow-job
Can fool the pants off any Russki polecat!

So you'll retain my vote, Bill!

You know just when to unzip in full view,
Pleasure yourself, while we voters just inhale.

What the U.S. Action Hero Needs

in this bloodless city-hell is to rise sharp,
before breakfast a life-and-death struggle
on the penthouse lintel, maybe a car chase
through an imploding downtown mall,
wrong-way joy-ride up a subway escalator,
elbowing crowds aside, expending
sub-machine gun clips wildly....

Maybe a leap between two rooftops!

bracketed by a spangling fusillade of Uzi fire,
along with a triumphant post-traumatic *cafe latte*
ripped from my lips by an unexpected shotgun blast.
Sure, I'd like *you* here too,
but no straight-backed scribbling lectures.
This time *down,* loaded with make-up,

a treat sprawled over the bed as wholeheartedly
open as only a Hollywood starlet can
when commanded by her Director
to simulate surrender to a charismatic chauvinist
with a killer twinkle and an erotic black shoulder sheath.

O reckless relentless love!

Later, if you like, slightly *triste,*
you can speculate on the problematic
effect of endless savage war and celebratory violence,
whether my feelings (or yours) shall long endure it,
stay awake to the unsuspenseful, unscripted
beauties of life and bridge our inevitable *difference.*
Just so long as we understand each other.

Like Evil, baby, androgens never sleep!

I dream hard and get up very late.

While Doing My Exercises

Out on the sun porch
the old pine rocker
catches a June gust and spins,
slim and beautiful.
On the cedar boards,
free for a moment
of the burden of others,
it capers and cavorts
while I, gasping
from my own weight,
jerk up alongside
from my push-ups to watch.

Blues Funk

Lyric verse, pah!
I could have been a Blues harp
contender!
svelte duck-tailed nomad
harmonica wielding windbag
venting slumped bug-house,
donut joint,
chipped beer glass misery
with(out) compare.

Writhing in a downtown
mock meat-loaf odyssey,
tapping out salt
from my dented nickel shaker
on the big slug's tail,
a life of clip-joint fare
and ware....

O Sonny Boy!
O Little Walter!
O Paul Butterfield!
Great late pantheon of blue!
O wannabe of musical despair!
O me!

Scribbler togged in day-job beige,
in dreams zoot-suited,
full pleated
gal-treated
blues-rooted
posed kitty-corner, ’hood mourner,
railbent dandy, gandy dancer,
carpet-cutting,
sucking,
executing deep bends true,
shed-dog howling,
big rig-honking....

Lift off the roof!

Redneck Genesis

From the bush back of roller coaster roads
pastures spill gleaming and anonymous
like snaps from fumbled garage sale albums.
In a box shaped clearing slumps a derelict trailer,
sag-backed by a kitchen tip from which protrude
broken tvs, dirt bike bits, a gold toy
World Wrestling Association Championship belt
in a final bout with rank gone-to-wild tulips.

The End of Our World

On this Earth, inherited for a song,
A finale, describing how we, humankind,
Smeared, bleared, blighted our Big Mom,
Till one sweltering, short-of-breath day,
She played the ruthless charlady with her kettle
And boiled us like a dooryard nest of ants,
Or torched us like a windrow of usurpatory
Lime-splattered starlings, then,
Humming a charming, restorative ditty,
Lightheartedly sashayed on.

Jack Sprat and His Wife

Brilliantly greedy woman
how you gorge on excess!
–it's passionate, chair-splitting, fat mess,

while I, your antipode and a confirmed
  belt shortener,
grow thin as a slat
–even eschewing
my fussily chosen, already frugal feast,
and slide *between* the chair and the table.

Still, dear, for both, the last
stop's the floor-
in a sort of cross-eyed, slumped disarray
  of more and less....

Among trim skirted calves and neatly
  creased legs
we exchange under-the-table glances,
wondering who
the other brilliant scapegrace is
–need hardly guess!

The Helots

By reflex slaves
we blink
at the downstroke
crash
of the regime's hammer,
eyes sealed to everything.

Now and then,
one of us,
eyes furiously watering,
nevertheless tries to look.
The hammer falls on him!

Chicago Harp Blues

To the late Junior Wells

Alley frost,
sharded, gleaming utterance,
a limo window blown
in long splinters
on crazed asphalt
in windy Muddy Waters Land.

Wibble-warble riffs
stacked chrome chords
like some flashy Seventies Nigger Caddy
swerving itself off,
hi-time jinking,
swoop-cruising
Chi-town's offay, Art-Deco Hennepin:
rubber-squealing,
backfiring,
passing pale-man faces
miffed by pimp-dream
nightmare cream,
gaudy toaster chrome trim....

O Junior, I done once seen him
but no more.... He dead, maybe gone!

From corner shoe-box to Southside stage, on....

Look Over Yonders Wall!
That hard crying-man!

Blues Spook, pull curbside.
Let me in.
Ear to your *Delmark* LP's in my downtown flat,
I accompany on my battered Hohner,
rhyme along in a monkey funk,
despair's jobber,
dream-busker,
tuning up my grief for virtual chump change
from plush camel hair coats:
right-wing blondes with perfect teeth,
passing Tits and Tippers.

Spider Bend

Where the Tomifobia hooks,
a rock maple tilts,
webs rigged over every crotch.

Rising daylight reveals
a full-sailed galleon!

From upriver, a dawn wind
gusts through the narrows,
rakes the bank ferns,

showers up night-dew,
clouds of drugged,
slowly spinning flies....

Spiders, like sailors, know the ropes.
White webs fill, gorge with bugs,
hungrily, like huge cheeks.

Nihil Admirari

For Keith Henderson

Above serial corderillas
of artfully folded Truth and Beauty,
above peaks topped by strivers, modelling
    the latest fibre-based, lightweight gear,
tilts that huge-winged, mountain vulture,
    Poetry.

September Campfire on the Gouin Reservoir

For Ber Lazarus

What does this hungry flame mean,
sulfur yellow, copper green,
on this dimming wild bay,
ravaging driftwood to twists of ash?

Spooning food from pots,
I wonder this as the red sun sets,
smoke flattening along the slim beach,
bright stars successfully edging a front

at a minnow sprinkle offshore
where a jack-fish eddies once, twice,
swims contentedly, thoughtfully on.

This Life

This long, winding riverbank
whitening in early May moonlight,
rollicking with ice-out,
black spruce foldings of ravine slopes,
half-blocking the grinding of tractor
trailers on highway 55....
Strange if this is it, stranger by far
than salvation or personal immortality.
Me, at twilight, picking my way
across a pale, ice floe littered plain.

Odd indeed, if this be *all,*
luminously meaningless, protean,
evanescent, sited in a Cosmos
like some endlessly unfolding, exploding diagram,

a fay keep raised in the marches of a diminutive
  yellow sun,
fey matter that only to itself matters....

Strange, weird, even appalling!
(Fear the only deity, first and last.)
But lovely too: delicate, animated,
glimmering like new lightning bugs in June,
or like that fog's incandescent sock,
there, lifting off the river bend,
thronging down towards the highway bridge
with patched abutments where, last year,
they fished out an old farmer, self-drowned.
I hardly knew him or he me, though once when
he caught me crossing his lots, rambling for no reason,
talking to myself loud, he just grinned.

Beauty, and at times a little companionship.
The moon sets, trail muck frosts,
truck noise drops. Time to turn back.
Under the sharp, plunging glitter, the swish of blood
in my head waltzes amid immense silence.

On the Subject of the Non-existence of Matter

Regarding Berkeley's Idealism: "I refute it thus."

Booting a rock to confirm obdurate materiality
the eighteenth century *Litterateur*
shuffled on (mighty grump)
his goal scored, pragmatic as water.

Good God! down here, all is stony;
ever rolling, stripped of mystical spagnum,
a place fallen and remiss. Starved and yearning,
we gnaw, like stooped reindeer, at sparse lichens.

What a harsh, unascended world this is!

Yet Dictionary Johnson, balloon puncturer,
this worldly realist, our intellectual superior,
one time voyaging among the Western Isles,
missed his spurs in an open boat.

They were iron, cast like small anchors,
yet, despite all appearances,
on and on at Boswell he railed:

"Surely, a wave has carried them off!"

Ornithological Mystery

The wild
duck's cry
leaves no echo.

None knows why.

Dark Asteroid

I dream of you
spitting from
heaven's black chops,
pip of Chaos, your
hooked mountains,
deep crevasses,
swarthy cheeks,
swooping down,
Semite nomad,
on the cities
of the plain.

Big Nose Kate, Lover of Doc Holliday, Reminisces

My fling with the Southern Dentist of Death,
It's reported, was tempestuous.
Lately some Eastern gal penned a romance–
All lies!–about how in thwarted passion
I once tried to pistol that consumptive lothario.
Well, maybe we tangled some–
A hunkie hooker and a doomed Georgia swell.
A dozen, maybe a thousand times,
I told him: Go to hell!
He was, of course, already there.

Also, the rumours about his questionable
Character ain't all off the mark.
Consumption didn't spiritualize him much,
Or make him *too* sweet. A tooth-yanker
Plagued by The Cough, he went West,
Gambled without limits, ready
To bet that worthless chip,
His own life, on a card flip.
Winning honest against some dumb
Texas drovers, he was even prepared
To cheat for the hell of it!
So you see, with his teal-eyed,

Terminally fatal charm, he could be hard
To share bacon with, let alone a rug:
A mule when right,
A wolf when crossed, especially
On big things, like Life, sonofabitch Fate, Love–
What he dubbed "the wasting diseases."

At the drop of a hat, cornered,
He'd jerk a Colt or blade;
Blast or cut, then grin and shrug!
He was a man-killer (and lady-killer) from hell!
Which is why, I guess, except for me,
That cold man Earp was his lone *amigo.*
(Doc once saved his life....)
True, we was split by the time of Tombstone,
What they call the OK Corral fight.
(Drunk, I popped a cap at him one silly time.)
They write I didn't see the shoot-out,
Was elsewhere, after some "tiff."
Wrong! I rode in secretly that night,
Crouched across the way in Fly's Photography,

Praying goddamned Doc would die, no live–
Somehow, some way put himself out of his misery.
But that morning Doc was dealing,
On his game, wielding a *sawed-off,* slyly grinning.

Yes, likely he began the ball.
Men said when the Clantons balked,
Doc gave things a shove with both barrels.
Then when Frank McLaury yelled
He'd got Doc in his sights, said Doc:
"Blaze away. You're a daisy if you do!"
He seemed to relish the slug's red graze.
He was some feller, I tell you!
For this gal at least, he was *it,*
Though I never saw him once more after that.
He went to hell till the late Eighties,
When The Consumption finally snuffed him
In a Colorado hotel. He died in bed.
"This is funny!" was the last words he said.

Battle Site, Minnesota

Everywhere, to the relic plains' horizon,
genetically improved Indian corn parades,
accompanied by its sister tribe: Soya.
Thumping my Ford down a back road,
I marvel at not spotting for leagues
a flying insect, let alone a bird.
Then a pair of wings! Another!
I pull into my destination, a tiny memorial
park where in 1864 Santee Sioux cut off,
besieged a column of U.S. Cavalry.

No facilities on site, only an inscribed historic marker:
the ambushers crept out from nearby Birch Coulee,
now conquered by arboreal succession: American oaks.
Another plaque announces a resuscitation of the lost
Long-Grass Prairie, cinder-trailed,
signed in a cruciform series of stations.
Here, then, the bugs and birds have trekked
to this sudden, diminutive, paradisaical retreat,
spectacular acreage of shoulder-high turkey and
cord grass, whiskery gramma, crowned and wreathed by
mauve blazing stars, blue vervain, white campion,

cornflowers, and alien tufted canada thistles.
Hordes of red-banded, gold-winged butterflies
cluster and flap, delirious with nectar,
after eternities of barren Monsanto voyaging.
How the local farmers must bitch!
"Finance a bug's Eden with our taxes?–No way!
The only good Wild Prairie's a ploughed one," they say.

Tromping around the battle-site (irresponsibly)–
Please stay on the gravel paths. Native grasses are fragile!
my shoes fill up with stowaway wild seeds,
the unowned subtext: *Don't spread farmers' weeds.*
Present and past abide in uneasy harmony.
I tell myself one teal-blue Great Plains day,
the Harvester will lie down with the bison,
the Redman with the Michelin man.
Meantime, passing strange how to such a disheveled,
disputed plot, farm boys hurry their girls
to start their own green shoots, pledging to
step out of their forebears' ruts and grids.
I can see their love couches in the bluejoint now.
Deer lays, I thought at first, but I'll warrant
around here no big game survives.

Battle Site, Minnesota

Mandatory, some spot to pollinate,
in hopes we don't awake to find our earthly estate
expropriated by our most ruthless foe,
ourselves: some lovely site to stray back to,
lament heroic battle the Natives lost
and we somehow failed to fight.
Where is the wild hay we pressed to perfumes?
Still here! Its old world forever gone,
along with Red Cloud and the buffalo.

Let us dwell then, you and I, amidst a kitschy
patchwork of productive wastes and nostalgic relics,
picking at genetically tampered bread,
clamber on occasion over forbidden fences,
do our best to empty our shoes,
exhibiting a modest disrespect for the rules.
Often we don't get along.
Those who say otherwise are rank fools.
The bones and bullets in this ground testify to it,
the latter, under cover of darkness,

illegally vacuumed up as mementos
by metal-detector-poking collectors,
some of them government parks employees.

Over a nearby fence a farmer waves at me,
the semblance of a frown on his face.
I'm trespassing off the path and on a rove!
On my second glance, he seems to approve
my tromping through protected wild plants.
"Hear this place is famous for an Indian battle."
He replies: "Even more for necking and screwing!
Round here they call it 'Rubber Park!'"
I laugh, bending to empty a cuff. "Sorry.
Wouldn't want these weed seeds getting into your rows."
"Let me worry about that," he says.
"They'll blow into my land anyway."

Ur Cur

In Parc Jeanne Mance, dog-owners
in signature fall woollens,
converse, swivel
with hands on hips, flirt,
while loosed from their leashes,
three dozen canine
epigones of *haute coiffure,*
wasp waists and shapely limbs,
hurtle in a yipping,
wide, loin-nipping ring,
chasing the urge to fly
the dog-show tent,
hurry-hump,
whelp an elementary, off-white mutt,
plain as any Third World waste-lot Rex.

The Ballad of Doc Holliday

"To die in The West"–American frontier song.

I'm expiring in The West,
Malingering on year after unanticipated year.
My disease must like this place,
A saloon in a raw deal hotel
On a desert bluff drilled for silver.

Tombstone, Arizona:
Flush with gamblers, bunco men, *Nymphs*
De Pave, and (happily) saps without number.
Ville of Sharpsters and suckers
(I deem myself both).
Sawed-off under my blouse,
Plus a tell-tale graveyard cough.

Hip-shot at bar or money table,
I am an evil-breathed goose.
Eyes empty as a ready noose,
I supervise a faro bank,
The only game they let me win or lose.
A darb at dice and cards,
(With a certain Hunkie string-along),
My pleasure's dealing to miners mostly.
(Cowboys I give a quick skinning.)

They're poor Cornish, Welshmen, Germans
Too scared to refuse my invitation.
(There're advantages to a bad reputation....)
I call them my "already dead and buried!"
And own a soft spot in my black heart for them.
I let them discover little streaks of luck,
At night's end, cave the gallery on them.
Sometimes not! It all depends.
They understand, dub me the Southern Doctor of Death.
(I've only had to snap a cap at one or two of *them*).
They know I don't shake 'em for the money,
Or even for a living!

Maybe for the hell of it?
Drinking, coughing, drinking,
Slapping the blood-sprayed pasteboards down,
Whisky and gun battle unavailing,
I make my killing.

Dad

Only in our last years, I called him that.
Before, it was "father" (as in soldier).
Almost from the start we were more distant
than a son and his begetter should have been.

When I was a kid, he once roared
down a mud-tracked kitchen floor
that I carried on like some hideous little stranger,
maybe even Hitler's rumoured son!
"You should know!" I fired back before the blow.
We were often damned hateful to each other.
I did not say we hated....

He was shell-shocked in battle.
His superiors, knowing the use of a loner,
trained him as a night-raider and killer,
then, for "R and R," hounder of suspected traitors.

Was I such a suspect?
Now that he is gone and I'm adrift
in the punctured dinghy of middle age,
I realize life's baleful dilemmas
require one to think sparingly on them:
call it combat hygiene.

Before he cut back toward the end,
he smoked two packs a day.
Still a kid, having crossed him in some way,
I would dream of fleeing him,
while blue tobacco smoke streamed
from the old shrapnel wounds in his legs and knees.

Father, farther....

Yet, other times in tearful dreams,
I search incessantly
for him to salve some childish hurt.
Unable to find him, I duck in
the hall cupboard, to feel good again
wrap myself in his smoke-scented blazers,
jackets, and overcoats, closer and closer.

Tantrums

Driving two hours from the city
with the lady-friend and her kids,
I'm wrestling with the rumple of a Townships'
dirt road, when the teen son,
coming to the country cottage under constraint,
starts cursing a blue streak at his mom.

The Past leaves deep ruts.
The boy's insolent mouthing-off
makes me gasp, my eyes go red,
but for once I bite my tongue,
jerk the steering wheel to lift
my right tire from a hole, fail,
with a thump, drop the left into another,
high-centering the car on a long downhill run,
battering the underside transmission bulge,
grinding the muffler to scrap,
so that I'm the one yelling and swearing,
as the minivan slews sideways,
wheels pluming up brook-water, moose-mud,
shudders to a stop in a shallow creek.

With the license of inexperience,
the youth from the backseat starts to howl
in wild I-told-you-this-would-happen ecstasy,
suggests (now!) we turn home,
at which point I lose what cool I've got,
screw my chin and scarlet jowls round, spit:
"You insolent, foulmouthed son-of-a-bitch!"

Suddenly I'm in the skin of my dad
when I got under his skin,
the kid who insisted he drive out of the city,
somewhere, anywhere green,
(the reverse of this homebody,
hammer-locked by Nintendo and Wrestle-TV),
who showed his contempt for suburban stay-at-home
patio barbecues by silent, adolescent smirking,
or skulking around the bungalow,
badmouthing, slyly undermining,
never getting quite what he deserved: a fat lip!

The Night before D-Day

In the next bed, the old guy confesses
he's certain this time his jig is up.
No more miracles will save his neck,
the job offer on the Isle of Wight
as Baron De Rothschild's gardener
that got him out of Berlin in '39,
his subsequent internment as an alien,
sentenced to exile in Canada,
except he left his suitcase on the dock, missed
the boat torpedoed in mid-Atlantic, all hands lost.
What tales of sheer survival he tells,
understandably voluble,
since tomorrow it's quadruple bypass time.

Just fine for his room mate!
Terrified by *his* surgeon's date,
he welcomes the opportunity (by default)
to be the quiet one, stoic,
the self-possessed younger man,
offering comfort in a yawing assault craft,
like some rock solid, firm-mouthed NCO
dispensing palliatives while oiling his Sten gun.
He exudes *sang froid,* has seen the movie,
does a triumphant acting job playing
Glen Ford playing Johnny Canuck,
flattered that the old guy seems to buy it,
almost ready to die too now.

To Hazel Walker

– d. 2003

A bush rambler even after dark,
I hike up the old rail berm to the narrows,
where the river sprints thick and glinting
over a black couch of slate.
Under the moon, a water-fog uncurls,
spirals like ghosts of the elusive Abenaki gods,
throngs downstream, in a thick rising plume,
to a silver-edged collector pool.

I always follow the caving bank there,
where sometimes a muskrat, this time a beaver,
startled, veers at the apex of a gilt edged "v,"
before plunging, tail-whomps the water:
Boom! In warning of either Man or Beast….
"I don't walk there alone at night,"
you once warned me. "There's wolves!"

Shuffling through sodden swale grass,
  I think:
Tonight, there's just me,
not the four-leggeds, since,

despite your lively folk fears, Hazel,
the wild dogs always hide from men:
leave tracks seen in daylight flecking the berm,
are spotted as night glitter or sometimes,
at the day's red edges, from the bush line
eyeing your tractor. They're shy,
elusive, swift. I see traces everywhere
and yet have only ever spotted one.

Hazel, have you joined them?

The Indescribability of Fear

Out in the long corridor
the stuttering echo of footfall
as the dawn-shift nurses hurry up and down;

the catarrhous whump and tinny purr
as this pre-op room's ventilator kicks in;
my rubber pillow reprising squeaking

insomniac songs. On the cuff of the sheet,
stiff as plastic, my fingertips
hopping, endlessly scratching,

bugs lapped by a huge shadow,
burrowing beneath one other in futility.

After the Operation: First Visitor

To Susan

Your hand
suddenly here
pressed on my green smock's breast.

Head full of wooze,
searching for my own,
I reach out,

only to feel
your knuckles' delicate range,
the smooth slopes of your skin.

"How are you doing?" you ask,
squeeze mine with yours.
I am unable to answer.

Testing for neurological response,
the attending nurse interrogates:
"Where are you? What day is it?"

I groan hotly,
exasperated at being distracted
from your warm hand,

your companionate hand,
wonderful and sweet,
a lover's tender hand.

Last Commando on His Deathbed

Haunted: by a rebellious youth's
collision with World Cataclysm,
rescued through voluntary induction
from return to the house of a petty
furrier father, who declined to pay
for his son's further education
since his others desired none....

Haunted: by three sorties
against the enemy,
the first an escape from humdrum
coastal defence by stepping up
for commando duty,
climaxed by a melodramatic Pinewood Studios
raid by rubber boat on Nazi occupied Norway.

Up beetling cliffs, then cross-country creep
under a blue freezing moon
to a truck-pool where, snipping wires,
one Tommy triggers the alarm–
two small desperate forces in a guardhouse
confined, submachine guns crashing at zero feet,
(three German dead, one NCO gut-shot), then

bloody retreat, my father humping his belly-ripped
bleeding sergeant, abandoning him at cliff's brink,
alone with a Webley pistol (for whatever purpose),

while survivors clamber down, push off
searching for the dawn submarine that failed to show,
paddling the risen German Sea to Scotland,
strafed by the odd patrolling Heinkel.

Haunted: by a second visitation,
assigned to more salubrious climes,
a coastal French chateau on a gay Saturday night,
packed with Vichy officials, their wives, and
their overlords,
sharp suits and chic taffeta dresses soiree-ing
formally and slightly woodenly
the way lackeys and their bosses will.
"To the *Fuhrer*" and "*Oui,* to France!"
when at the door commandos in cork black
thrust in, snatch one, murder others,
then just to prove they aren't poopers
toss two trigger-wired Sten guns in
to dance upon the high gloss floor their fiery,
crashing fandango, till no party-goers remain
on their feet,

except for one French mayor, hustled off,
select chap, who after careful interrogation
in the pick-up submarine (punctual this time)
finds himself escorted up on deck by a youth,

not unconvinced of his innocence,
likewise in the service of two masters, who promptly
dispatches him with a new replacement Webley.

Haunted: a stern and introverted loner,
now detailed to less taxing, "lighter" Home Isles duty,
the wilder marches: Wales, to detect, neutralize
"misguided" Celts furtively furnishing to the enemy
petty secrets, burst local water-mains,
the mysterious break-down of the village clock....
(How did Jerry radio know that?)

Insinuating himself into the traitor's society,
accosting him at the pub, buying pints,
swapping appealing personal tales, until one blurry,
sentimental evening, the suspect's guard
completely dropped,
my father, eyes lit like Norwegian ice,
slides coat off a hard grey gun and whispers,
"Isn't it time you did away with yourself,
so we don't have to?"

Still in youth's flower, at twenty-six,
he finally cracks, blacks out supervising
mortar instruction at Aldershot, wound
    in his superior's greatcoat,
marches across the live-fire range, garden
    of thundering blooms.
After plucking him from certain death,
they book him for court-martial, then
perceiving he's deranged, place him in hospital.

Haunted: even now, dying in bed at last,
    face moon-ashen,
doggedly hopeful, body time- and war-worn,
ever a commando, grimly stoic, battered,
("They want another CAT-scan of my bones.
    I can't imagine why!")
waiting now before a small dark guard post,
to kick the door, dive in, commence a Sten gun
duel with The Enemy at point blank range.

Born in Coventry, England, Steve Luxton lives in Montreal and also near Ayers Cliff in the rural Eastern Townships of Quebec. By profession a teacher, he works at John Abbott College and Concordia University in the city. An original editor of both *Matrix* and *The Moosehead Review,* his first completed book of poems *the hills that pass by* was published in 1987, and his second volume *Iridium* in 1993. *Luna Moth and Other Poems* is his third full collection.